A LOOK AT CONTINENTS

EXPLORE ASIA

by Veronica B. Wilkins

pogo

Ideas for Parents and Teachers

Pogo Books let children practice reading informational text while introducing them to nonfiction features such as headings, labels, sidebars, maps, and diagrams, as well as a table of contents, glossary, and index.

Carefully leveled text with a strong photo match offers early fluent readers the support they need to succeed.

Before Reading

- "Walk" through the book and point out the various nonfiction features. Ask the student what purpose each feature serves.
- Look at the glossary together. Read and discuss the words.

Read the Book

- Have the child read the book independently.
- Invite him or her to list questions that arise from reading.

After Reading

- Discuss the child's questions. Talk about how he or she might find answers to those questions.
- Prompt the child to think more. Ask: There are many different climates in Asia. What is the climate like where you live?

Pogo Books are published by Jump!
5357 Penn Avenue South
Minneapolis, MN 55419
www.jumplibrary.com

Library of Congress Cataloging-in-Publication Data

Names: Wilkins, Veronica B., 1994- author.
Title: Explore Asia / by Veronica B. Wilkins.
Description: Minneapolis, MN: Jump!, Inc., 2020.
Series: A look at continents | Includes index.
Audience: Ages 7-10 | Audience: Grades 2-3
Identifiers: LCCN 2019031182 (print)
LCCN 2019031183 (ebook)
ISBN 9781645272885 (hardcover)
ISBN 9781645272892 (paperback)
ISBN 9781645272908 (ebook)
Subjects: LCSH: Asia—Juvenile literature.
Classification: LCC DS5 .W457 2020 (print)
LCC DS5 (ebook) | DDC 950—dc23
LC record available at https://lccn.loc.gov/2019031182
LC ebook record available at https://lccn.loc.gov/2019031183

Editor: Susanne Bushman
Designer: Michelle Sonnek

Photo Credits: Extarz/Shutterstock, cover; Mc 243/Shutterstock, 1; Viktar Malyshchyts/Shutterstock, 3; Nguyen Quang Ngoc Tonkin/Shutterstock, 4; Shutterstock, 5; Maciej Es/Shutterstock, 6-7 (foreground); Jaroslav74/Shutterstock, 6-7 (background); Vixit/Shutterstock, 8-9; HelloRF Zcool/Shutterstock, 10-11; Gueffier Franck/Alamy, 12-13; Jim Cumming/Shutterstock, 14 (foreground); al_nik/Shutterstock, 14 (background); ewastudio/iStock, 15; David Steele/Shutterstock, 16-17; DONOT6_STUDIO/Shutterstock, 18; Tavarius/Shutterstock, 19; Fotos593/Shutterstock, 20-21; Eric Isselee/Shutterstock, 23.

Printed in the United States of America at Corporate Graphics in North Mankato, Minnesota.

TABLE OF CONTENTS

CHAPTER 1

ASIAN LANDFORMS

Let's explore the **continent** of Asia! Beaches line the southeast coast. Ha Long Bay is full of **islets**. They have rain forests on top!

Ha Long Bay

Lake Baikal is in northern Asia. This is Earth's deepest lake. It is more than 5,000 feet (1,524 meters) deep! It is the only place on Earth to see Baikal seals!

Asia is the largest of the seven continents. The **equator** runs through the far south. Most of Asia is in the Northern **Hemisphere**. Some islands are in the Southern Hemisphere.

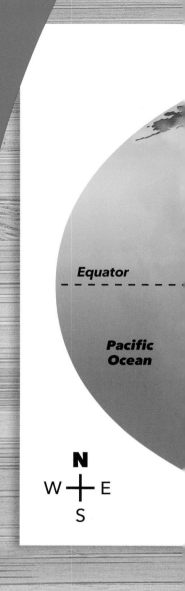

Equator

Pacific Ocean

N
W E
S

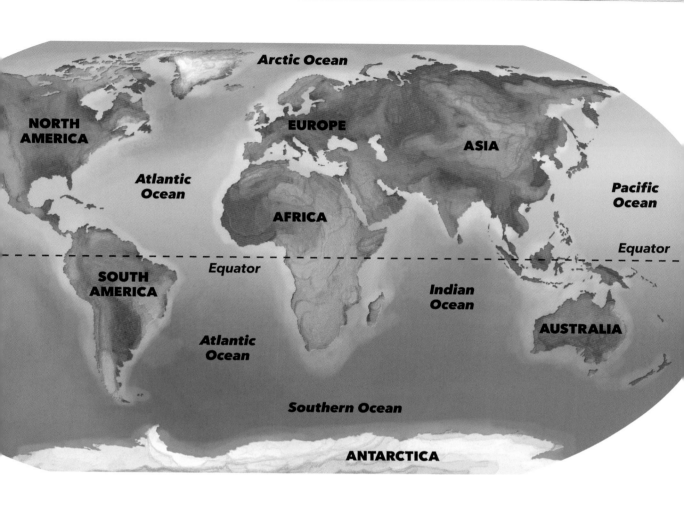

Arctic Ocean

NORTH AMERICA

EUROPE

ASIA

Atlantic Ocean

Pacific Ocean

AFRICA

Equator

Equator

SOUTH AMERICA

Indian Ocean

AUSTRALIA

Atlantic Ocean

Southern Ocean

ANTARCTICA

Mountains cover about 75 percent of Asia. The Himalayas cross the center. They contain Earth's highest point. Mount Everest is 29,035 feet (8,850 m) tall! People travel from around the world to climb it.

WHAT DO YOU THINK?

Climbing Mount Everest is very hard. It is also very dangerous. Why do you think this is? Would you like to climb this mountain?

Mount
Everest

Plateau of Tibet

This is the **Plateau** of Tibet. Some call this area the roof of the world. Why? It is Earth's highest plateau. It is surrounded by mountains. Yaks live here. They eat the grasses. Their long hair keeps them warm.

Asia includes many islands. Some have active **volcanoes** on them! Mount Sinabung is one. It erupted for the first time in around 400 years in 2010. Now, it is one of the most active volcanoes in Asia. It is in the Ring of Fire.

Mount Sinabung

TAKE A LOOK!

There are many volcanoes in the Ring of Fire. It is around the Pacific Ocean. What other continents does it touch? Why do you think it is called the Ring of Fire?

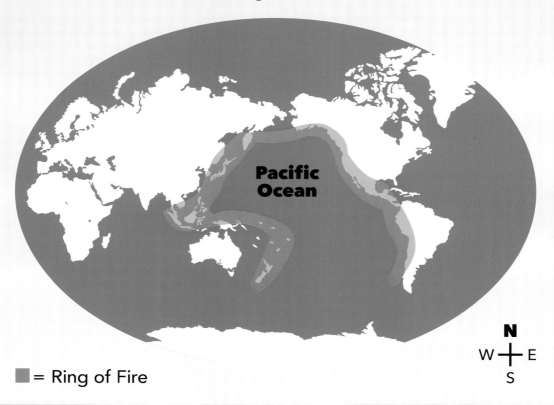

Pacific Ocean

N
W — E
S

■ = Ring of Fire

CHAPTER 2

MANY CLIMATES

There are many **climates** in Asia. The north is **polar**. Arctic fox and reindeer roam.

Tigers prowl the south. It can be hot here! Why? It is close to the equator. There are two seasons here. They are the rainy and dry seasons. The rainy season brings **monsoons**.

Central Asia's climate is more **temperate**. But mountains here have snow on top. The Middle East has many deserts.

TAKE A LOOK!

What are the climate **regions** of Asia? Take a look!

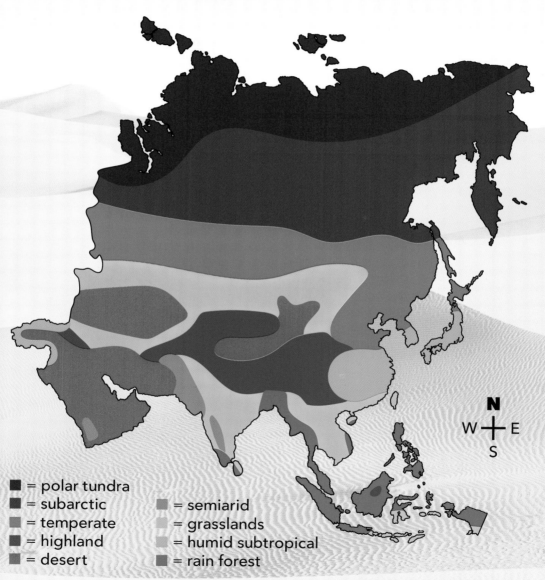

- ■ = polar tundra
- ■ = subarctic
- ■ = temperate
- ■ = highland
- ■ = desert
- ■ = semiarid
- ■ = grasslands
- ■ = humid subtropical
- ■ = rain forest

CHAPTER 3
LIFE IN ASIA

More than half of Earth's **population** lives in Asia. Many live in **rural** areas. Farming is common. Rice and tropical fruits are popular **crops**.

China and India have the largest populations on Earth. Shanghai is one of China's largest cities. More than 34 million people live here!

Shanghai, China

Singapore

Singapore is an island in the south. Many people **immigrated** here from across Asia for jobs. Many **cultures** come together in the city's busy streets.

There are many climates and sights to experience in Asia! Would you like to explore this continent?

WHAT DO YOU THINK?

Many languages are spoken in Asia! Money in India can have as many as 17 languages on it. What language do you speak? Would you like to learn more?

QUICK FACTS & TOOLS

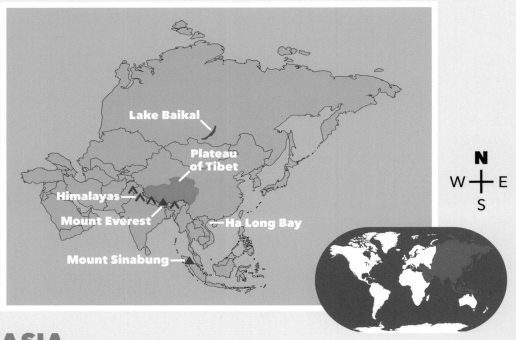

ASIA

Size: 17,226,200 square miles (44,615,653 square kilometers)

Size Rank: Asia, Africa, North America, South America, Antarctica, Europe, Australia

Population Estimate: 4.7 billion people (2019 estimate)

Exports: rice, petroleum, manufactured goods, software

Facts: Asia makes up about 30 percent of Earth's land.

Russia and China, two countries in Asia, are larger than the entire continent of Australia.

GLOSSARY

climates: The weather typical of certain places over long periods of time.

continent: One of the seven large landmasses of Earth.

crops: Plants grown for food.

cultures: The ideas, customs, traditions, and ways of life of groups of people.

equator: An imaginary line around the middle of Earth that is an equal distance from the North and South Poles.

hemisphere: Half of a round object, especially of Earth.

immigrated: Moved from one country to another and settled there.

islets: Very small islands.

monsoons: Seasons or storms that bring heavy rain.

plateau: An area of level ground that is higher than the surrounding area.

polar: Near or having to do with the icy regions around the North and South Poles.

population: The total number of people who live in a place.

regions: General areas or specific districts or territories.

rural: Related to the country and country life.

temperate: A climate that rarely has very high or very low temperatures.

volcanoes: Mountains with openings through which molten lava, ash, and hot gases erupt, sometimes violently.

INDEX

TO LEARN MORE

Finding more information is as easy as 1, 2, 3.

1 **Go to www.factsurfer.com**

2 **Enter "exploreAsia" into the search box.**

3 **Choose your book to see a list of websites.**

FACT SURFER